University Cornell

Proceedings at the unveiling of the tablet to the memory of Louis Agassiz and at the formal opening of the Sibley College extension

1885

University Cornell

Proceedings at the unveiling of the tablet to the memory of Louis Agassiz and at the formal opening of the Sibley College extension
1885

ISBN/EAN: 9783337196493

Printed in Europe, USA, Canada, Australia, Japan

Cover: Foto ©Andreas Hilbeck / pixelio.de

More available books at **www.hansebooks.com**

CORNELL UNIVERSITY.

PROCEEDINGS AT THE UNVEILING
OF THE TABLET

TO THE

MEMORY OF LOUIS AGASSIZ,

AND AT THE FORMAL OPENING OF THE SIBLEY COLLEGE
EXTENSION, AND THE UNVEILING OF THE

PORTRAIT OF THE HONORABLE HIRAM SIBLEY.

JUNE 17, 1885.

PUBLISHED BY ORDER OF THE TRUSTEES.

ITHACA, 1885.

Table of Contents.

I.

LOUIS AGASSIZ.

II.

HIRAM SIBLEY.

THE SERVICES OF LOUIS AGASSIZ

To the Cornell University and to Science.

Among the events of most lasting interest that marked the seventeenth Commencement of Cornell University was the unveiling of the tablet placed in the Founders Chapel by the Trustees of the University in memory of Louis Agassiz. The exercises were held in Sage Chapel, on Wednesday afternoon. The account of the proceedings which follows is unfortunately incomplete, inasmuch as the remarks of Mr. James Hall, and ex-Governor Alex. W. Rice were delivered without notes, and as no stenographic reporter was present they have not been preserved.

In opening the proceedings, President White alluded to the great services rendered by Professor Agassiz in the early days of the University. He stated that among those of whom he took counsel frequently regarding the organization of scientific instruction and the claims of candidates, Agassiz was most helpful.

At the opening of the University in 1868, Professor Agassiz was present and made one of the speeches upon the occasion, entering most heartily into the new enterprise, pledging it his support, and giving most valuable hints on its proper line of development. Immediately after he began a course of twenty lectures before very large audiences including nearly all of the student body. They made a deep impression upon all who heard them, and gave a strong impulse to scientific study and research which has literally remained a power for good in the University from that day to this.

Many of the young men who received that impulse in Agassiz's lecture room at that time are now occupying Professorships at Cornell and elsewhere throughout the country, especially in the universities, colleges, and normal schools of the west. To the end of his life Agassiz constantly showed proofs of his attachmènt to the University, and nothing could be more fitting than the tribute paid him to-day.

Brief addresses were then made by James Hall, State Geologist, and Professor J. S. Newberry, of Columbia College, in behalf of Professor Agassiz' former co-workers ; and by Professors T. B. Stowell of the Cortland State Normal School, P. R. Uhler, of the Peabody Institute, Baltimore, and B. G. Wilder, of Cornell, in behalf of Professor Agassiz' former students and assistants. A few of the numerous letters of regret received from prominent scientists and educators were read by Professor M. C. Tyler.

A dirge was then played upon the organ in the chapel by Professor Flagler of Auburn, during which a procession was formed. This then marched to the Founders Chapel where the President of the University uncovered the tablet, and the Ithaca Quartette sang *Integer Vitae.* The inscription on the tablet reads in black lines as follows :

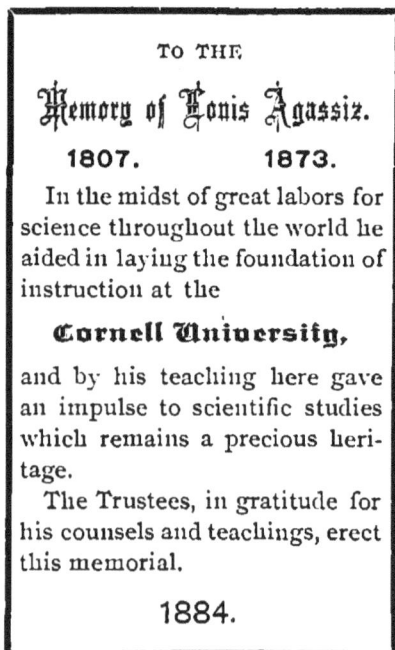

TO THE

𝔐emory of 𝔏ouis 𝔄gassiz.

1807.   1873.

In the midst of great labors for science throughout the world he aided in laying the foundation of instruction at the

Cornell University,

and by his teaching here gave an impulse to scientific studies which remains a precious heritage.

The Trustees, in gratitude for his counsels and teachings, erect this memorial.

1884.

LETTERS OF REGRET.

The following letters of regret were read after the remarks of President White.

BOSTON, June 9, 1885.

MY DEAR SIR : I regret that it will not be in my power to visit Ithaca and be present at the unveiling of the tablet in memory of Louis Agassiz. My relations with the illustrious professor were of long standing and always most cordial and to me delightful. It would be a great pleasure to me if I could be with the friends who are to do honor to his memory. We have borrowed distinguished men from the old world before his day. France lent us Lafayette. Germany spared us Steuben to lead and to discipline our armies. Switzerland had already sent us Albert Gallatin, the counsellor of Washington, the statesman identified with the history of the Government for more than half a century. He was still living when his fellow-countryman, Agassiz, reached our shore to blend his life with our American civilization as unreservedly as did the great financier, diplomatist and scholar who had preceded him.

The special work of Agassiz was to establish the scientific independence of his adopted country. The dream of his ambition was to make the favored centres of the New World strong enough in their attractions to draw students from the older schools of Europe. No pent-up Utica could limit his aspirations. No, not even your wide-margined and wide-minded Ithaca could have filled the large measure of his magnificent ideals.

"How much money would you really like for your museum?" I once asked him.

"Ten millions," was his instant answer.

This enthusiasm spread among all with whom he came in contact. Students followed in his steps as the disciples of a new religion tread in the tracks of their teacher. His eloquence led captive the most obdurate assemblies, the least tractable of listeners. The purses of rich men opened like the mouths of his cyclostomata. The hard-featured country representatives flocked about him as the fishes gathered to listen to Saint Antony, as the birds flocked to hear the sermons of Saint Francis.

It is in vain that we should try to describe his fascinating personality, the memory of which must fade away with this passing generation. But his noble contributions to science will keep his name in lasting honor, and the vast museum which he founded will be his proud monument as long as science has its altars and its priesthood in our Western hemisphere. I am, dear sir,

Yours very truly,

OLIVER WENDELL HOLMES.

HON. ANDREW D. WHITE, *President of Cornell University.*

NEW HAVEN, June 3, 1885.

DEAR PRESIDENT WHITE : It would give me great pleasure to comply with your invitation to take part in the Agassiz Memorial Exercises at your University, but it is my misfortune to be unable even to be present. Agassiz of all men of Science is the one I most like to honor, both for what he was, and what he did for American Science. My heart went out to him with strong affection; and I rejoice that your institution will commemorate his connection with it and his great service to Science in a memorial tablet. Thanking you for your invitation, I remain

Sincerely yours,

JAMES D. DANA.

HON. ANDREW D. WHITE, *President of Cornell University.*

—

(Translation).

42 GARDEN ST. CAMBRIDGE, Mass., June 4, 1885.

PRESIDENT A. D. WHITE.

DEAR SIR : In reply to your kind invitation to be present at the ceremony of the 17th inst, in memory of L. Agassiz, and even to make some remarks, I regret to say that for several years I have been an invalid. I never leave Cambridge, and it is impossible for me to attend any public ceremony, even the regular meetings of the American Academy of Sciences at Boston.

I am happy to learn that Cornell University is the first public institution to do justice to and honor him, who has done more for zoology and the glacial theory in America, than any other scholar.

I am the last survivor of those who came to the United States with him or on account of him (except Lesquereux, who, however, did not arrive until several months after our return from the exploration of Lake Superior, during the summer of 1848). This is enough to show the interest which I take in everything that can recall my regretted and illustrious friend.

Very respectfully yours,   JULES MARCOU.

—

NEW YORK, June 4th, 1885.

DEAR SIR : Your kind invitation to attend the unveiling of a tablet commemorating the services of the distinguished geologist and zoologist Louis Agassiz, just received. I regret that the distance is so great as to preclude my attending, or at least of giving a definite promise ; but permit me to express my appreciation of the act you are about to perform. Certainly the great name you are about to honor is one intimately associated with that of the University ; and while the influence of Agassiz extends to every American college whose organization includes a biological department, Cornell University may be said, in the person of one of its Faculty, and a leading pupil of the Swiss professor, to have inherited from him in the "direct" line beyond all others. Thanking you for the compliment, I am

Sincerely yours,

E. C. Spitzka.

Andrew D. White, Esq., *President Cornell University.*

—

Letters of regret were also received from Professor Asa Gray, of Cambridge, Mass. ; Dr. Harrison Allen, of Philadelphia ; Mr. J. A. Allen of the American Museum of Natural History, and lately of the Museum of Comparative Zoology ; Professor S. F. Baird, Secretary of the Smithsonian Institution ; Harlan H. Ballard, Principal of Lenox Academy, and organizer of the many Agassiz Associations among young people ; Professor E. W. Blake, of Brown University, formerly of Cornell ; J. Henry Blake, Artist Naturalist at Cambridge ; Professor E. W. Claypole, of Buchtel College, Ohio ; President Eliot, of Harvard Univerisity ; E. A. Gastman, Superintendent of the Illinois Board of Education ; President Gilman of the Johns Hopkins University ; Rev. Dr. Thomas Hill, formerly President of Harvard University ; Professor J. B. Holder, of the American Museum of Natural History ; President D. S. Jordan, (Cornell, '72) of the Indiana State University ; Professor Joseph Leidy, of Philadelphia ; Professor E. S. Morse, of Salem, Mass. ; Professor J. T. Rothrock, of Philadelphia ; Professor S. H. Scudder, of Cambridge, Mass., editor of "Science ;" Professor N. S. Shaler, of Harvard University ; Professor S. I. Smith, of Yale College ; Professor A. E. Verrill, of Yale College ; Professor H. A. Ward, of Rochester ; Mr. W. J. Youmans, editor of the "Popular Science Monthly," and others.

ADDRESSES.

Mr. President, and Ladies and Gentlemen :

It is evident, that no one, however gifted, could satisfactorily perform the duty which has been assigned to me on this occasion, namely, in ten minutes' time to give an exposition of the life and labors of one of the most individual and interesting of men, and one of the ablest, most distinguished and most useful of scientists. But it was my good fortune to enjoy for nearly thirty years the friendship of Agassiz ; and I should be ungrateful to him and untrue to my own feelings, if, when opportunity offered, I failed to express, though in broken phrases, my admiration and gratitude.

My special craze, as some of you know, is geology, and among the different departments of this science, perhaps the subjects which have interested me most have been fossil fishes, and the Ice Period,—that most mysterious and dramatic chapter in our geological history. Agassiz was best known as a zoologist, but he was also an eminent geologist ; his interest in science was in fact universal, and his range of knowledge phenomenal. His most important published work was his *"Recherches sûr les Poissons Fossiles,* in which he gave figures and descriptions of all the fossil fishes known up to the time of its completion, and by this and his work on the Fossil Fishes of the Old Red Sandstone, he may be said to have created the science of fossil ichthyology, This was a subject in which he felt the keenest interest up to the day of his death ; and when, a young man, I brought to him some of the remarkable fossil fishes I had found in Ohio, he received me with more than cordiality, and from that time all the rich material he was accumulating in the Museum of Comparative Zoology, and all the stores of his vast knowledge, were freely offered and often used in the prosecution of my studies.

Although Agassiz's most voluminous works are those on fossil fishes, and these gave him world-wide celebrity among scientists, his studies of the glaciers and the surprising results of those studies have contributed more to his popular fame.

In 1815, Charpentier, the Director of the Salt Works at Bex, and one of the most distinguished geologists of Switzerland, passing a night in the cottage of a mountaineer in the hamlet of Lourtier, was told by his host that he believed that the glaciers had formerly a much greater extent than at present, because, as he said, "I find huge boulders of Alpine granite perched on the sides of the valleys, where they could only have been left by ice." This remark excited the interest of Charpentier and was practically the beginning of the investigations which have resulted in the theory of the Ice Period. In 1834, Charpentier brought before the Association of Swiss Naturalists at Lucerne a report upon the evidences of the former extension of the Swiss Glaciers, the result of his observations through many years. At that time a group of young, able, and enthusiastic scientists were gathered at Neufchatel,—Agassiz, Guyot, Schimper, Desor, Carl Vogt, Wild and others. The new theory of Charpentier that ice had once filled all the Swiss valleys, excited in them the greatest interest, and they devoted themselves during seven successive summer vacations to the thorough investigation of the facts upon which it was based. Agassiz here as everywhere was leader, and inspired the others with his irresistible enthusiasm. He devoted himself especially to a study of the phenomena presented by the modern glaciers, their mode of formation, the character, measure and cause of their motion, etc. Practically he lived on the glaciers during the summer months, and part of the time occupied with his assistants a cave under a large boulder on the Aar glacier which was long known as the *Hotel des Neufchatelois*. Guyot devoted himself to the study of the record of the glacial flood in the Swiss valleys furnished by the boulders carried on the surface and deposited along the edges of the ice, tracing with great sagacity and perseverance the high-ice line over the Alps and Jura till he had mapped out all the ancient glaciers.

In 1837 the Association of Swiss Naturalists met at Neufchatel, and Agassiz then advanced the theory of a general glacial epoch of which he may justly be called the author. At first it met with violent opposition, but this only stimulated those who had adopted it to greater enthusiasm in their researches. Ultimately it was demonstrated that not only had Switzerland been affected by an epoch of glaciation, but the Scandinavian Peninsula and the British Islands, so that the glacial theory was generally accepted for Europe. Agassiz proclaimed his belief that it would be found equally applicable to the whole northern hemisphere, and one of the motives which led him to come to America was his ardent desire to see for himself whether the glacial record was the same for the New as for the Old World. So, almost as soon as the steamer which brought him reached its dock he hurried to the hills that surround Massachusetts Bay, and there to his great delight in the *roches moutonnés* and beds of boulder clay, found proof of the former presence of glaciers which no one had previously recog- nized. In Maine, Massachusetts, and other parts of New England he continued his observations until he had worked out all the generalities of the history of the Ice Period in eastern North America. At the same time he inspired an interest in the subject which set many others at work on the problem, and it was soon found that the Ice Period had left here its most impressive record, and that at its maximum, fields of ice and snow reached down to New York, Cincinnati and St. Louis, enveloped all the highlands of the West and indeed occupied fully half the continent. Many years before his death Agassiz had the satisfaction of knowing that his theory was applicable to the whole northern hemisphere, and had the pleasure of studying in southern South America a similar though perhaps not synchronous record.

The results of the glacial studies of Agassiz and his associates have never been fully published, but the most important of the observed facts and the inferences deducible from them are given in his *Systeme Glaciere* and *Etudes sûr les Glaciers*, the most im- portant contribution yet made to the abundant literature of this subject. These splendid works, with his monographs on fossil fishes, his Natural History of the United States and other publica- tions, constitute a monument to his ability and industry which should satisfy the ambition for scientific fame of any man ; but enviable as is the lot of one who has ability and opportunity to make such investigations and leave such a record as he has con- tributed to science, still the publications of Agassiz, voluminous as they are, constitute the least important part of his life work. It is a splendid thing to have the time, the ability, and the means to write and publish an exhaustive monograph upon some important subject of research. This serves not only as a guide and help to other workers, but is the most enduring and glorious monument to his own fame. But to write a monograph is not the highest achievement of the human intellect, nor the richest fruit of human life. The teacher who educates hundreds and thousands of workers, and stimulates the production of perhaps as many monographs through other hands, does a greater work than the solitary and possibly selfish specialist who spends his time exclusively in building his own monument. So, too, the founder of a school, like Aristotle, Cuvier or Agassiz, does a greater work in the promulgation of his system of philosophy and the inspiration of his followers and pupils, than by any individual contribution he may make to literature. However valuable and important we may reckon the writings of Agassiz, all who knew him and his work must concede that the grandest achievements of his life were as a teacher of science, and that his highest claim to our honor and admiration is in the noble institution, the Museum of Comparative Zoology, which he founded ; in the enthusiasm he excited and the methods of research he inaugurated among the young men who were his pupils, and in the general impetus he gave to scientific studies in America. Only those who know what science was when he came among us, can realize the potency of the influence he exerted. In the earlier years of our national existence our people were naturally occupied in the practical work of founding a nation and achieving the material conquest of a continent, and time and taste for abstract thought and scientific investigation only came when the rough work of civilization was accomplished. Only in the last half of the century of our national existence have art, literature and science gained general recognition among us as worthy objects of thought and effort. When Agassiz arrived in this country forty years ago he found us just aroused to the importance of these subjects, and he appeared among us as the apostle of the new gospel of science. He spoke our language fluently and even elegantly, while a marked accent only added piquancy to his speech. Wherever he went his characteristic enthusiasm was contagious, and a personal magnetism which surpassed that of any other man I have known, made an impression which was not only wide-spread but deep and indelible. His Lowell lectures upon zoology were attended by people of all ranks and avocations, but they were alike inspired with an interest in the subject which was unexpected and unprecedented, his vivid descriptions and remarkable facility in drawing captivating and delighting all.

In 1848 the American Association for the Advancement of Science was organized, and for many years Professor Agassiz was a constant attendant upon its meetings. These were held in turn in all the principal cities of the United States. Those who were present at any of the earlier meetings will not fail to remember what a vitalizing, animating element Agassiz' presence was. The effect of these annual scientific reunions in different places was most potent in giving to science an honorable position in the estimation of the inhabitants. Wherever they were held the hands of the local workers were strengthened and the ranks were recruited with new men. Academies of science, geological surveys, and scientific professorships in colleges followed as natural results. Any one can see by looking over the list of papers read at these meetings what an active part Agassiz took in them, but no record remains except in the memory of those present of the wonderful inspiring and formative influences he exerted, which warrants us in crediting him with a large part of the good accomplished by this, the most potent of all agencies in the science culture of the country. Later Agassiz was one of the moving spirits in, we may say the inspiration of the movement for the organization of the National Academy of Sciences, and was its foreign Secretary until his death.

I have now touched upon some of the salient points in the character and career of Agassiz; have given you an all inadequate sketch of this interesting man, and this grand, noble and fruitful life, and I have consumed the time alloted me. Yet I venture to ask your indulgence for a moment longer while I report an incident in the intercourse between Agassiz and myself which is not without interest and suggestion. As I have said one of the most important of Agassiz' achievements was the establishment of a school of science at Cambridge, and the education of a large number of young men to whom he imparted his enthusiasm and his scientific methods. These young men are now scattered over the country, each diffusing in his own circle the light kindled from the spark of Agassiz's genius. Among these are Morse at Salem, Putnam and Hyatt at Cambridge, Packard at Providence, Verrill at Yale, Wilder here at Cornell, and others, who are continuing the work which Agassiz inaugurated, gaining fame for themselves and for the institutions with which they are connected, by their usefulness as teachers and their success as investigators. In this category I should not forget to mention Alexander Agassiz, on whose shoulders his father's mantle so worthily rests. By his researches in invertebrate zoology he has shed new luster on the great name he bears, and he is devoting the wealth, which fortunately for science has come to his hand to the fulfillment of his father's plans. Nor can I omit those whose brilliant careers have been cut short by death.—Burnett, Stimpson and Clark. Between a number of these students and Agassiz an estrangement had at one time occurred and they had left his school and were located for the most part in Salem, Mass. In 1869, a meeting of the American Association was held at Salem, and Professor Agassiz, who had withdrawn from it, was induced to be present, and resumed his membership and friendly relations with his old students. At the close of the meeting I offered a resolution of congratulation and of thanks to Mr. Geo. Peabody for his munificence in the endowment of the Peabody Academy of Sciences, just then fully organized and placed under the control of Agassiz' former pupils. In the remarks offered in support of the resolution, after expressing high appreciation of the admirable equipment of the institution, and returning thanks on behalf of science to Mr. Peabody, I took occasion to specially commend the scientific work which had been there commenced, and said that in its methods and spirit I recognized the hand of a master, that inasmuch as Professor Agassiz had inaugurated the train of causes that had culminated in this institution, and his influence now pervaded it, I felt that he deserved equal honor for its success. The resolutions were passed by acclamation in the midst of great excitement. Agassiz rose to express his appreciation of the compliment, but he was overcome with emotion, tears filled his eyes, his voice failed him ; soon recovering, however, he responded with great warmth and his usual felicity of language. After the adjournment of the session, he came to me to express his personal gratitude for my kind words, to which I replied that I had there said little of what I felt, and that as he was an older man than myself I should perhaps outlive him ; in that case I would endeavor to do fuller justice to one whom I regarded as not only a great light in science, but a benefactor of humanity. In his characteristic, dramatic way he clasped his hands with the ejaculation ''Why can't I die while you are in that mind ?'' We little thought that I should so soon be called upon to perform the duty to which I then pledged myself. On December 14th, 1873, he died from cerebral congestion, in the full possession of his great powers, and in the midst of the activities by which his strength was always overtasked, and to which it finally succumbed.

As President of the New York Academy of Sciences it became my duty to announce this irreparable loss to science, and I then took occasion to review at greater length than I could here do his life and work.

I now further fulfil the promise which I made to him living, by offering this imperfect tribute to his memory.

ADDRESS OF PROFESSOR T. B. STOWELL, OF THE CORTLAND STATE
NORMAL SCHOOL.

Mr. President :

It is a proud moment in the life of any student of Professor Agassiz, when he is permitted to give expression to his regard, his love for his honored teacher ; to pay tribute to the memory of his revered dead.

Such is my privilege to-day. I would not presume to stand in this presence to recount the traits which distinguished Professor Agassiz as a man ; to rehearse the proofs of his eminent scholarship ; or even to mention the genial nature which endeared him to all ; for I see those whose acquaintance extended over years as my own embraced weeks ; his co-workers, his intimate advisers, his confidential friend ; to these is properly referred the pleasing task. I cannot, however, refrain from voicing some of the many recollections of Penikese, which crowd upon my mind.

It was most natural for a teacher to study Professor Agassiz as a teacher ; from this standpoint he presents strong characteristics. I have for years regarded Professor Agassiz as the founder of a system of instruction in this country, which has done more than any other agency to modify and to revolutionize the fixed methods of the schools. This feature is embodied in the reply once made by the Professor himself, when asked "What do you regard as your greatest work ?" "I have taught men to observe."

It is true that objective teaching was introduced and advocated long ago ; but Agassiz more than any other man brought to the attention of American educators the superior merits and claims of objective work.

The school at Penikese was opened and conducted upon the theory that objective work is the only basis for scientific research. Those not present at this school can form only a meagre conception of the character and the amount of work accomplished; and even those who were most actively engaged in the work of the school have had scarcely time to comprehend the magnitude of the enterprise. It has pleased some of the jealous critics of American scholarship to speak lightly of this work: but I do not hesitate to say that an equal array of talent, of special scholarship, of zeal to discover, and of devotion to science, has never been witnessed in any other school in the history of education. It is the equal pride of instructors and of those taught, that our beloved Professor, whose memory we revere, stood among his associates at Penikese, unrivalled, without a peer.

The work at the Island Laboratory, like the work at the Museum, disclosed many traits of character which must ever remain an inspiration to all who were privileged to come in contact with them.

Professor Agassiz was an ideal educator by virtue of the scope of his scholarship. A question was never raised by an inquiring student without his receiving in return such an insight into the relations which were involved, that years of continued research alone

have enabled the student to comprehend the full scope of the reply.
Professor Agassiz represents the model teacher because he knew
subjects, and not merely about subjects. His references were not
to opinions and conjectures, but to things themselves ; the former
he knew, he was not a stranger to the latter. Professor Agassiz was
eminently an educator by virtue of his characteristic enthusiasm.
We meet men, who are able by charm of voice, or grace of presence to awaken interest in the cause which they espouse; it is rare
to find one who implants the germs of an enthusiasm which develops
and strengthens with the years. His presence never chilled, it
awakened new interest ; with his absence he did not withdraw the
inspiration which had been in-breathed by his presence.

Professor Agassiz was America's greatest educator by reason of
his unselfish devotion to the discovery and the promulgation of
scientific truth.

Penikese was the outgrowth of this element in his nature. Many
earnest students were toiling with indifferent success because of
their lack of acquaintance with scientific method and with scientific results. Professor Agassiz saw this source of embarrassment,
this hindrance to the growth and spread of truth. His own delight in the study of nature, his firm conviction that such study
was most effective in giving scope to scholarship induced him to
open this school for training observers. The correctness of his
theory, the wisdom of his course, the demand for such a school,
the magnitude of the undertaking, are all demonstrated in the mul-
tiple summer schools all over the country. Life is being studied
to-day with a zeal, a devotion hitherto unknown.

I believe that I do not overstate the truth when I claim that this
directing of attention to the study of nature is tracable to the im-
mediate influence of the school at Penikese. Summer schools by
the sea, summer schools by the lakes, at the universities, at
summer resorts are the direct offspring of the great school founded
by our lamented teacher.

I must allude to the crowning trait, Professor Agassiz's reverence. The problems of life which he sought to solve brought him
into such close communion with their author that he seemed to unveil the mystery; in every form of life he saw his Father's handi-

work. He shall rest enshrined in the affections of his pupils, the friend of nature, the friend of man, the friend of God, the student's best friend.

ADDRESS OF MR. P. R. UHLER, OF THE PEABODY INSTITUTE, BALTIMORE.

Mr. President, Ladies and Gentlemen :

On a bright, warm morning in the month of May, 1864, I called for the first time at the home of Professor Louis Agassiz, in Cambridge, Mass. Upon entering the house, I was directed into a small room at the side of a wide hall, which was plainly furnished and provided with a sofa and chairs covered with green worsted rep. It was an occasion of moment to me, for I was now to place myself in personal relations with the master who from that time should direct my energies into channels of his own selecting. He had invited me to come to his museum, to be his assistant in caring for, increasing, and arranging the extensive collections of Articulates which he had already assembled, and also to take charge of the scientific library belonging to the same institution. In a few minutes he came running into the room, and I stood before a man of massive build, having full chest, and broad shoulders, supporting a large head with high sloping forehead and prominent nose. The majesty of such a presence was overpowering ; but in an instant he had so completely placed me at ease by his cordial, engaging manner that I felt I had indeed found a friend.

He was about to take his accustomed walk to the post-office, and invited me to accompany him. Speaking in his kind, enthusiastic way, he told me somewhat of the progress he had made in securing collections of insects and allied creatures, representative of the great areas of geographical distribution; how many species were restricted to certain depths in the oceans ; how others were confined entirely to altitudes above a given line ; and how some forms had been spread forth from a particular spot where they had been created, and now occupied a definite region beyond which they could not successfully extend. This lesson was not lost upon me, for I had previously read everything that he had published in America, and had spent such time as I could command in testing his theories by the facts, as far as I could reach them, in the field, and in the study.

It was to be my duty to amass specimens especially of insects, to arrange some of them in systematic series, others in faunal series and still others as types of groups for the use of teachers in the public schools. He advised me to take every opportunity to acquire a knowledge of the range of variation in species, and to try to discover the reasons for the plan of structure of the articulate type. His frequent visits to my room in the museum, gave me an opportunity to become better acquainted with his great mental grasp, and almost intuitional perception of the fundamental principles of structure in a group. The most elaborate outer covering of details failed to hide from his keen vision the basis of construction which rested beneath. His versatility, enthusiasm, and desire for more specimens of natural history appeared to have no bounds. No price nor trouble seemed too great to expend when coveted collections were needed to fill out his plans for a universal museum of representative species.

The American continent had for him a peculiar charm. He loved its mountains, plains, and waters, and every object connected with them, whether living or fossil. Every pebble and bit of shale had a story for him; the simplest insect, as well as the most complicated animal, alike spoke to him of an intelligent plan in creation, of which he rejoiced to be the interpreter. Every region of North America was expected to contribute its representative species for study and exhibition in his museum. Consequently, each assistant was encouraged to make frequent excursions to the most promising localities, to secure the forms belonging strictly thereto. One of these short trips resulted in a very pleasurable surprise to me, which perhaps you will pardon me for reciting. The salt-marshes of Eastern Massachusetts are well provided with forms of insect life. In midsummer, when the tides fail to cover these wide areas of low surface, multitudes of small, rather flat insects, belonging to the Hemipterous genus *Salda*, inhabit the wet mud and damp sand there. They constitute separate species of three or four sizes and of different colors. The largest is of a deep uniform black, a smaller size is tan-brown, a third is almost uniform sand yellow, and a fourth is black, marked with small white spots. On Cape Cod there is a fifth species which is almost all white on the upper side. Now when I showed all these forms to Professor Agassiz (who was previously unacquainted with them) and referred to the distinctions in their colors and patterns of marking, he at once asked me where I had found each kind. Upon being told that they were taken from the salt-marshes and adjoining beach, he immediately remarked that they represented different areas of distribution, and that each variety of color would be found to correspond with the color of the soil. I need hardly say that this latter fact had already been established before the specimens were shown to him.

Such little incidents of slight importance in themselves, will suffice to show the quick insight of the master naturalist, and the ripe experience which he brought to the solution of new problems of natural history.

To me, Professor Agassiz was always a kind, instructive master, delighting to communicate his impressions with regard to any question that was selected for study, and ever ready with a word of encouragement when the problem seemed too obscure and difficult to solve. His fertility in devices for securing a hypothesis by which to test facts was to me a frequent surprise ; and a desire to reach truthful results in every pursuit of knowledge, was persistently present in his methods. With all his great craving for the best and most of everything that contributed to a knowledge of natural laws, he was ever ready to help with counsel and personal influence, and sometimes entangled himself in embarrassing engagements to aid in carrying out some broadly conceived plan of investigation. But on the other hand he hated dishonesty of word or action, and while he was keenly sensitive to indifference or neglect of duty, he punished peculation by the prompt dismissal of the peculator.

Three years of study and labor, frequently beneath the eye of this great instructor, taught me the grandeur and loftiness, as well as the fine texture of his manly nature. The friendship which he felt for those who were earnestly committed to the development of his life's object—a museum which should display to the eye the order of creation and reveal the thoughts of the Creator as therein expressed—was deep and lasting.

— 22 —

Our great Teacher (and he loved to be known by this name) has gone from us; but he has left an imperishable legacy of his spirit to encourage us to go forward in the paths of study which he so ardently pursued. Agassiz came to us and lifted the natural sciences out of the obscurity in which our earlier naturalists left them. We owe to his courageous intelligence the best and highest thoughts, if not the most subtle generalizations, which have been evolved from a study of the animal kingdom.

His museum, upon which he spent the best energies of his incessantly active mind, is the most thorough exponent of animated nature that has yet been produced for the instruction of humanity.

ADDRESS OF PROFESSOR BURT G. WILDER.

Mr. President :

Those whom it has been our privilege to hear this afternoon have shown you Louis Agassiz as a collaborator, as an investigator, and as a teacher. Permit me to corroborate what they have said, and to speak of him more as a man and a patriot, as a counsellor and friend.

Born a Swiss, and already in the prime of life when he reached this country in 1840, Agassiz became an enthusiastic American. Not only did he refuse tempting offers from the Old World, but he became a legal citizen of the United States at a time when some already such were fleeing from new and heavy responsibilities. In the dark days of 1861–62, Agassiz took out his naturalization papers, and bade God-speed to those of his students who entered the union army.

With a breadth of view which enabled him to plan what it will require years to execute, Agassiz had a remarkable facility in attending to details. In 1868, (while in Washington, co-operating with Professor Baird in persuading Congress to permit the withdrawal of alcohol from bond for scientific purposes without payment of tax), he wrote a letter respecting the work to be done at the museum during his unexpectedly prolonged absence. Ten persons were mentioned and for each was laid out work in continuity with what had been done already. After careful specifications as to matters relating to anatomical preparations, drawings, classification and geographical distribution the letter concludes : "See also that William [the errand boy] is busy and does not loaf about. I have directed him to make skeletons of cats, rats and mice, many of each kind."

His working habits were simple in the extreme. His private room was rarely occupied. The specimens and books he wished to examine were usually on a plain table in the common room, and in the few hours he could snatch from overwhelming administrative duties, he never seemed so happy as when, resting a foot upon the stool which at other times served him in place of a chair, he held in one hand some Brazilian fish and with the other turned the pages or plates from which to determine questions of identity, affinity or distribution. While thus engaged he sometimes whistled very softly a little air the source of which I have never ascertained.

Besides his writings and his museum, which are at once his monument and his legacy, we of to-day are materially benefitted by Agassiz' personal influence upon the sentiment of the community. Thirty years ago the following is said to have occurred : A summer party of Harvard professors were driven through the White Mountains. As the coach slowly ascended a hill, Agassiz and others would leave it and presently return laden with stones and wild flowers, or ornamented with beetles and butterflies pinned to their hats and the lappels of their coats. Professor Felton sat alone in the coach perusing a favorite Greek author. "Who are those fellows," at last asked the coachman, in whose eyes plants were interesting merely as food for his animals, minerals as likely to impede progress, and insects as apt to interfere with personal comfort. "They are a party of naturalists" said Felton. "Ah !" replied he, "that accounts for it, poor fellows." A few days later he drove another party, to whom he confided his experience as follows : "Last Thursday I had the queerest lot of passengers you ever saw ; they were men grown and dressed like gentlemen ; but they kept jumping out of the coach, and like little children ran about the field chasing butterflies and bugs, which they stuck all over their clothes. Their keeper told me they was *naturals*; and judging by their conduct, I should say they *was.*" Then, the great naturalist was taken for a harmless lunatic ; but he persisted and the people at last listened to his precept and followed his example. And if, to-day in almost any part of the United States, a man may pursue living creatures otherwise than for sport, and talk of them for another object than passing an idle hour, and nevertheless retain the respect of the community ; if in short the occupations of natural history collecting and teaching are now honorable and at least more lucrative than before, it is to Agassiz more than any other one man that the change must be ascribed.

The one man Agassiz did the work of four. He was an investigator, and a promoter of research, a popular teacher and the founder and curator of a great museum. What had he in return ? Besides the pleasure of doing, a pitiful stipend, a most laborious life, and a premature death. But for continual overwork and anxieties, most of which could have been arrested by the financial support which—matchless beggar though he was for others and for science—he neither asked nor gained for himself,* he might be speaking to you to-day in person, rather than through his friends.

If his life may be held up as a splendid example, his death, at sixty-six, twenty years too soon, should be regarded as a solemn warning to the enthusiastic naturalist not to drive his too willing horse, himself, to death, and to the community and those who represent the community in the control of educational funds, not to delay the practical recognition of a man's value until he is claimed elsewhere or until death makes repentance too late. Agassiz left us before his time because he did too much for us and we too little for him.

On the 8th of August, 1873, but a few months before his death, speaking of the recent loss of a valued assistant, Agassiz said : "My time will come soon, and I am ready." How many of us can say that with sincerety?

---

*In 1869 he wrote me : "Every year I am less inclined to work for money," and I know that when he did, the sums so hardly earned were expended not for personal comfort or in providing for the future, but in the purchase of specimens or in the employment of others to do what he had not time to do himself.

His published writings, his private speech and his daily life gave assurance of his faith in a wise and tender Father, but he would not discuss dogmas, and repelled as an impertinence the too common American fashion of inquiring what church a man attends. Twenty five years ago there was much less readily than now admitted to be a distinction between ecclesiastical observance and religious belief so that, while criticised as a bigot by some scientists, Agassiz was attacked by some theologians as an infidel, because he could not reconcile the facts of geology with the ordinary interpretation of the literal sense of Scripture. He did not deny that the Bible may be the Divine Word ; he simply confessed his personal inaptitude for unravelling its mysteries; but he did feel that, without presumption and with some hope of success and usefulness, he might devote his life to the exposition of that other revelation of God to man, Nature.

Did he succeed? Yes, and No. To the truth, the overwhelming truth of the affirmation, your speakers have borne witness to-day, and none will dissent. But can any mortal hope to accomplish all that he undertakes? If Agassiz was not the leader of zoologists in all things as he was in some, it was, in my humble judgment, because he failed to recognize the compatibility of sentiments such as he entertained respecting the Creator with an acceptance of the general idea of evolution. The question is too great for discussion now. But perhaps—as one who had imbibed from Agassiz a decided aversion to any derivative hypothesis, and who became an evolutionist only when forced to decide for himself what should be said to earnest and thoughtful students—I may express the belief that, if Agassiz could have taken something from Darwin, or Darwin could have taken something from Agassiz, a perfect and colossal interpreter of Nature would have enlightened the world. Then would the scientific scoffer have speedily become extinct, and of working naturalists, the few—the very few, not the ninety-nine out of a hundred as recently claimed by a sensational preacher—who still hesitate, would have been converted long ago to the grand, composite faith, at once natural and spiritual, that, by some kind of evolution, as yet far from fully understood in its

details, the earth and its inhabitants have been brought out of
chaos and formless matter. I will go a step farther. Agassiz
and Darwin were not personally hostile. Early in 1871 the
former wrote me as follows: "I have read both volumes of
Darwin's 'Descent of Man,' which he sent himself, with a few
very pleasant words. You know that we are truly friends, much
as we differ in views." Without abating a jot of my reverence for
him to whom I owe so much, I like to think that now, in that
other life, in that better world where all clouds have passed away,
Agassiz and Darwin are at one in belief as to the methods of creation, as they were united here in searching after truth.

Weighted from an early age with labors and cares which over-
taxed even his great powers of body and mind,the tenderer side of
Agassiz' nature was not seen by all. A single incident may show
the readiness with which it could assert itself. For a certain piece
of work an elderly German artist had come to Cambridge, leaving
a large family in a western city. When his absence promised to
be longer than at first anticipated, to relieve his loneliness, the old
man sent for one of his children, a lad of ten. Supplied with
credentials of various kinds, the boy reached Cambridge, and was
directed to the house of "Herr Professor." It was after dark, and
Agassiz sorely needed rest, after a long day at the museum.
Yet—instead of sending a servant as some would have done—he
did not hesitate to take the child by the hand, walk several
squares, and deliver him to the anxious father.

Did time allow, I would gladly speak, as might a son of a noble
and loving parent, concerning other features of Agassiz' many-sided
character as they were unfolded to me, especially after the summer of
1866, in somewhat intimate relations which were never for a moment
marred by disagreement or loss of mutual confidence. Let me
close by reading a passage from his Humboldt Address* which not
only contains the key-note of his own life-purpose, but also ac-
cords with the views and action of our president : †

*Address delivered on the Centennial Anniversary of the birth of
Alexander von Humboldt, under the auspices of the Boston Society
of Natural History, September 14, 1869.

†The Message of the Nineteenth Century to the Twentieth. An Address before the class of 1853, Yale College, June 26, 1883. The Irving
Literary Bureau, I, No. 28.

"The physical suffering of humanity, the wants of the poor, the craving of the hungry and naked, appeal to the sympathy of everyone who has a human heart. But there are necessities which only the destitute student knows ; there is a hunger and thirst which only the highest charity can understand and relieve, and on this solemn occasion let me say, that every dollar given for higher education, in whatever department of knowledge, is likely to have a greater influence upon the future character of our nation than even the thousands and hundreds of thousands and millions which have already been spent and are daily spending to raise the many to material ease and comfort."

PROCEEDINGS AND ADDRESSES

AT THE FORMAL OPENING OF THE

SIBLEY COLLEGE EXTENSION,

AND THE UNVEILING OF THE

PORTRAIT OF THE HONORABLE HIRAM SIBLEY.

At 2.30 on Wednesday afternoon of Commencement week, Trustees, Faculty, Alumni, students, invited guests and others assembled at Sibley College, for the formal opening of the building, as it had been enlarged and improved through the munificence of Mr. Sibley. After the brief ceremonies attendant upon the opening, a procession was formed headed by President White and the Hon. Henry W. Sage, for the inspection of the new museums, laboratories and machine shops. This completed, the procession under the charge of Lieutenant Schuyler marched to Gymnasium Hall.

The portrait, a finely executed painting by Huntington, was then unveiled by President White, who referred to the history of the Mechanic Arts Department, and paid fitting tribute to those who had been instrumental in its development. The Hon. Erastus Brooks then spoke for Mr. Sibley; Walter C. Kerr, Esq., for the Alumni; the Hon. Alonzo B. Cornell, and the Hon. Stewart L. Woodford for the Trustees.

The following pages contain these addresses. Music by Parlati's orchestra concluded the exercises.

ADDRESS OF THE HONORABLE ERASTUS BROOKS.

I have been reminded, Mr. President, since I entered this beautiful hall this afternoon, that I am to speak for Mr. Sibley. I have neither gifts, nor knowledge, nor grace of language, thus called upon, to do fitting honor to the office entrusted to me. Looking upon this portrait, I may say in the language of Milton,

" Come, then, expressive silence muse its praise,"

for in the silence of the portrait more than in the language of the speaker you may find a fit recognition of the great service Mr. Sibley by his many gifts has rendered to Cornell and to the State at large. In my knowledge of men I know of no man who would better illustrate the rise and progress of the American nation than the founder of this University and those who, like Mr. Sibley, have been associated with him in promoting great public work in the establishment and building up of great universities ; and I hope I do not trespass upon the office which I hold, when, in the dim future I see, and in faith believe that Cornell is to be second to none in any of the States of our most prosperous and favored country [applause]. And no man of the present time has contributed more in a practical way and for a practical purpose to the present necessities of the country in the promotion of the mechanic arts, —"the blacksmith's hammer and the woodman's axe ;" and no man is doing more in the saving of time—time being money, —time being prosperity, and time in this rapid age of ours means that men seem to live longer in results in a year than they lived in a score of years in times that are past—I say I know of no man who better illustrates the rise, progress, and prosperity of the American nation, than Hiram Sibley. Born among the poorest of the poor, one of a family of fifteen with remarkable peculiarities, inheriting but indigence, but with indigence a large intelligence and thrift, with a zeal that never faltered, a courage that never failed, and with a hope as boundless as life itself, he loved industry, thrift, and enterprise, and was in all these qualities an example to all men around him. Such men never fail.

This portrait better than any words I can express illustrates the man whom we honor to-day. Here is the image of the man, yonder (pointing to Sibley College) is his monument—giving in its completeness an illustration of what an institution like this can do, of what this institution has done and is doing, to promote the industries of the country, and to give an example to young men everywhere.

But I must be brief, knowing the length of the appointed exercises of the day, and I will only say of Hiram Sibley in his absence, what I will not venture to say in his presence, knowing his dislike of all praise :

"May he live longer than I have time to tell his years,
Ever loving and beloved may his good name be ;
And when old time shall lead him to his end,
Goodness and he fill up one monument."

ADDRESS BY WALTER C. KERR, ESQ., IN BEHALF OF THE ALUMNI.

Mr. President and Gentlemen :

As construction is the root of engineering, and the result, so is reconstruction largely the measure of progress; and in this ceremony of respect and gratitude to the honored benefactor of the Department of Mechanic Arts, I am glad also to echo the sentiments of the Alumni upon the recent progress made possible by the same liberal hand.

Those of us who first came upon this scene ten or more years ago can well appreciate the developments— the material extensions whereby one hour now replaces two, thus doubling the students' stock in trade. We, who crowded around one forge which was forced to do all grades of work can look with enviable pride upon the new smith shop with its ten well arranged fires. We, who together constructed machines from purchased castings with heavy turning, finished, and all but the lighter planing done in a neighboring railroad shop, can well realize the necessity out of which has grown the foundry and the new shop with its largely increasing and growing equipment.

We also find drawing tables where light is ample and where the jar of machinery does not add vibration to the already complex lines.

The devices heretofore ranked as models have been relegated to distant shelves, and ten times their space occupied by a collection worthy of the name—not equalled in this country nor excelled in any other.·

Many similar improvements directly in the line of accumulation around the nuclei of the past are visible on every hand, but in addition we are pleasantly confronted with new departures long desired and now realized. The Experimental Laboratory begins its important functions with the coming term and under auspices which render it impossible that it should be second to any in the land.

Coming rapidly, systematically and with the characteristic energy of this institution, its managers and its benefactors, these things are even more marked and more potent for good than if brought piecemeal between long stages of inconvenience and incompleteness. The impression produced and sustained is that the department is in its every action progressing, reconstructing, and in its effect meeting the demands of the times. Honor be to him through whose generosity this is possible.

In present prosperity we should not underrate the past. A natural tendency to so underrate springs from seeing before us many things which have heretofore existed only in our catalogue of wants. I venture the opinion with confidence, that the graduates of this department have obtained as large a percentage of what they desired as they can reasonably expect in any department of life ; certainly more than is realized in the average results of business undertaking ; certainly a greater ratio than the professor's salary bears to his reasonable expectations ; surely equal to the proportion of the engineers' contemplated achievements that are fulfilled. If any have been so alive to the needs of the department as to hastily adopt inexpedient methods of expressing opinion, let me here state positively that such actions can only be properly criticised as being an exponent of too ardent a zeal. If any have appeared indifferent, the cause has chiefly been an indisposition to co-operate with methods adopted by their fellow graduates, of which methods they did not approve. To-day I can say that the Alumni stand a united earnest body with all differences of opinion or method harmonized, and all equally willing to second every good move.

In crediting the past with its due, the unceasing afforts of those who have labored faithfully are kindly remembered. He who for sixteen years has carried the burden of responsibility for the efficient management of a department in a University, which department had no defined policy, or at best an imperfectly defined one, which University had not then the ready means to warrant the expense attendant upon properly defining a policy, who has borne the burden throughout the many vicissitudes of fortune and who has economically husbanded the necessarily limited appropriations for its maintenance, deserves and has from the Alumni an expression of their highest commendation for faithful performance of the task. Nor is the efficient work of one who spent seven years of valuable time for our good, in the past, forgotten through his absence.

The records of the Alumni of this department augur well for those who possessing greater advantages are to follow us. Omitting details let me say that those who have strictly followed Mechanical Engineering have done well. It is a source of regret that a number have followed other paths. This is in part due to individual circumstances and in part to the fact that the department necessarily remained one of Mechanic Arts according to original interpretation of the Charter long after it should have become one of Mechanical Engineering. This transformation now effected needs no further comment than to draw conclusions from the record. Chief among these is the fact that the success of the graduates indicates the demand of the world upon the department.

It has always been a fixed purpose of Cornell University to send out men to fit the times. Our lately established departments of History and Political Science and Electrical Engineering clearly indicate this policy. Twenty years ago educators and practical men of the world were deliberating upon the nature of a department which should represent the proper interpretation of "those branches related to the Mechanic Arts." The interpretation then made was believed to meet the demands of the time and was accepted without criticism. After twenty years the question again arises and is settled in accordance with the times more easily than before, yet not without room for difference in opinion. Twenty years hence the same problem will again arise, and then, as now, we can thank those who drew our charter for the liberality of the requirements, allowing any needs to be filled within the range of interpretation.

We now enter upon the era of Mechanical Engineering proper, by way of development rather than direct creation ; with the way paved by those who have conducted the instruction in the past, with the opportunity afforded by the wise decisions of the honored guardians of the University ; with the project made possible by the munificence of him to whom we pay just tribute, and with the plan carried to full completion by one who comes to us as a master of all comprehended within the worthy title he bears.

To those present who are to enjoy the advantages now offered I would like to say much ; but this is not the time or place. I would however mention two things which form the most common subjects for discussion in your curriculum. They are shop work and higher mathematics. Consider skill in the former not as an end, but as an important means to an end. Consider familiarity with the latter a great labor saving machine. In all your work cultivate habits of concentration, accuracy, and decision. It has been truly said that " in engineering a man gets paid for what he can do, not what he knows," to which I wish to add, that his value depends quite as largely upon the responsibility he can safely assume. Lastly, and particularly remember that no amount of genius can take the place of hard work.

Technical education has received a great impulse in this country from Cornell University, and no technical department has more opportunity to practically demonstrate the effect of such education, than that of Mechanical Engineering. The time is ripe, the demand exists and there remains much to be done by those who thus prepare for the doing. The expense of efficient conduct is one of the greatest problems in the matter. High grade work must be maintained and commercial efficiency, so necessary in engineering, must be exemplified by the very atmosphere of the Department. To this end the equipment must be as ample as is that of efficient manufactories. Able leaders and assistants there must be

as in the world of practice. We now take a fresh start with fair
complexion, on a larger scale than even the most sanguine have
anticipated ; but depreciation must not be ignored. A manufac-
turing plant keeping pace with the times is duplicated every ten
years or an expense equal to duplication is expended for maintenance. The requirements of an engineering department parallel
with the times must fully equal those of the manufactory, and it is
the hope of every Alumnus that the good work of this department
and its graduates shall be so manifest that those who provide for
its welfare shall fully realize its needs in constantly maintaining
the important work it has to accomplish.

Reviewing the past and contemplating the present, realizing
what was given us and what now stands open to those who can ob-
tain for the asking, our gratitude goes out to Hiram Sibley in such a
way that to formulate it in words is to weaken it, and it is only in the
work we accomplish that the full expression of our thanks can be
made. Mechanical Engineering has not been an educated profes-
sion, and this fact makes wide the field for those who at this time
enter upon it with the preparation which is the basis of efficient
work. On this account the energy expended in thus training
young men to-day and the money spent to successfully equip and
carry on such a department draws compound interest and will
continue so to do for generations.

The Sibley College of Mechanic Arts is a pioneer in the work,
and I can only present to-day the handful of young men whose
best work is yet to be done ; but when time has passed and long
after this portrait we now unveil has been decorated with the
wreathes of many anniversaries, a greater wreath of works, not
leaves, and as broad as the land shall be woven about it and the
weavers will ever proudly bear honor to him whose name is insep-
arably linked to the foundation of their success.

Mr. President :

Never before has my inability to address an audience been the
cause of so much regret as upon this occasion when it would af-
ford me so much pleasure to make an adequate expression of my
appreciation of him whom you have to-day met to honor. My rela-

tions or rather my associations with Mr. Sibley extends back over a period of thirty years, coveting all of the time since the organization of the Trustees of this institution and ten years prior in which we were closely connected in the telegraph service. In all of these years our personal relations have been of the most cordial and friendly character and time has only served to increase my respect for him.

Mr. Sibley commenced life as a poor boy without any of the advantages of position or wealth and literally made his own way. By industry and energy he made himself master of whatever task fell to his lot and often accomplished results where others less resolute would have given up in despair. He accumulated considerable wealth in commercial pursuits and at an early day became associated with others in the development of the telegraph interests of the country. He was the master spirit in the great enterprise of extending telegraph lines across the continent and bringing our Pacific coast within the range of electric communication. Later he was largely engaged in the construction of our splendid railway system and has also been identified with other important business ventures. In many ways he has wielded great influence and has accumulated a vast fortune, a very liberal portion of which he has devoted to the cause of higher education, not only in establishing the department here of which you, sir, have spoken so eloquently, but also in the building of an elegant library building at the University of Rochester. Beside these he has built churches, founded schools, and indeed it is impossible for me to recount half that he has done in these directions.

The department which Mr. Sibley has founded here at the Cornell University is calculated to exert an important and beneficent influence. It will lead the young men who come here to a new departure in the way of education, and will fit them for better work, enabling them to avoid the beaten paths of competition, in which men are treading so closely upon each other's heels as to leave but little margin for profitable employment. Perhaps an illustration of the advantage of directing young men just commencing life into fresh channels of employment may be given by a single word in reference to this locality. Within forty years there

went forth from this county of Tompkins thirty or forty young men
to engage in building telegraph lines and the development of that
great enterprise.   Upon the thumb and fingers of one hand can be
counted those who went from here whose fortunes—or at least
whose estates, for some of them are no longer in this life—are to-
day of more value than all the assessed valuation of the real and
personal estates of the entire town of Ithaca.   These young men
were thus led off into a new branch of industry and they accomplished grand results.   Just so Mr. Sibley's endowment here will
lead other young men into original fields of enterprise and give
them opportunities which would otherwise be beyond their reach.
Within the past ten years we have witnessed many wonderful
developments in the uses of electricity.   The invention of the tele-
phone has added more than fifty millions of dollars to the wealth
of our country while that of the electric light has added millions
upon millions.   These and similar inventions are to be improved
upon and supplemented by the young men who are to be educated
in the Sibley College of Mechanic Arts.

ADDRESS OF THE HONORABLE STEWART L. WOODFORD.

The programme tells us that at four o'clock this afternoon
the unveiling of the Agassiz tablet is to take place at the Chapel.
The hour has passed, and we are still here admiring Mr. Sibley's
picture and recounting his good deeds to our University.   If,
however, you wish to carry out the programme and attend the exercises at the Chapel, it is your good fortune that my regard for the
truthfulness of the official circular compels me to be very brief.

Memory goes back to-day, Mr. President, over the years that
have passed since the thought of this University first took shape.
That thought has never been better expressed, will never be better
told, than in the language which Senator Morrill used in the original charter, the bill passed by Congress giving public lands to
colleges.   He said that the gift was to establish colleges "where
the leading object shall be, without excluding other scientific and
classical studies, and including military tactics, to teach such
branches of learning as are related to agriculture and the mechanic
arts, in order to promote the liberal and practical education of the
industrial classes in the several pursuits and professions of life."

With large wisdom our State confined to one college the lands that thus came to New York. With great generosity a citizen of Ithaca gave half a million dollars to secure the location of that University here in Ithaca. With singular good fortune there were associated with Ezra Cornell, a body of men who made the realization of this idea possible. There was John McGraw who is now gone ; there were Hiram Sibley and Henry W. Sage who are still with us. These were four men who had never been inside college doors. But they were men who had learned the practical power of science. They were men who, without early education, had undertaken great enterprises, which required a high order of mechanical training and scientific knowledge. They were men who had made great fortunes for themselves, and who said : "Others, no matter how poor they are, shall have better advantages than we had when we began, so that they may do better work than we have been permitted to do." Thus Cornell University was founded. Thus has it grown.

The builders of Cornell were fortunate in bringing to their help and aid a wise and cultured although young man who knew what was meant by higher education in its best and truest application. Cornell was fortunate in its founders. It has been equally fortunate in its first President. Thus under the guidance of men who had made their own fortune and of a man who, having inherited a fortune, had given his life to educational work, they built this University. Labor, science and the highest education have mingled and wrought together, laying the foundations deep and broad, and building upwards towards a high and ever higher ideal.

To-day that dream is realized. We stand within the arsenal, on the site of a great military school. Behind us stretch the broad acres of our college farm. Yonder at the further end of the Campus is the great mechanical college, and between, is Founder's Chapel where to-day you will unveil the name of one of the great scientists of the land.

On this beautiful hill, under this golden sunlight, and amid these pleasant breezes of the early summer, we can say to-day that all which Ezra Cornell dreamed has been more than fulfilled, and yet we feel and know that what is here to-day is only the incomplete suggestion of the larger results that shall be here to-morrow.

www.ingramcontent.com/pod-product-compliance
Lightning Source LLC
Chambersburg PA
CBHW021603270326

41931CB00009B/1353